Game of Thrones:

The Ultimate Game of Thrones Character Description Guide

(Includes 41 Game of Thrones Characters)

David Nolan

Table of Contents

Introduction to Game of Thrones

Game of Thrones is a fantasy drama series made for television, and airs on HBO. The television series is based on the series of novels authored by George R.R. Martin, named A Song of Ice and Fire. The name of the television series has been adapted from the first novel of the series, called A Game of Thrones.

The series follows several plotlines, which are intertwined and interweaved with each other. The main story line follows the seven major kingdoms engaging in civil war in order to claim the right to the throne, while another plotline explores the threat of the upcoming winter and the undead creatures from the North.

The series has been lauded by various critics worldwide as one of the best shows on TV right now. It has already won several awards and nominations from prestigious bodies, which include the Emmys, the Golden Globe Awards and even a Peabody award. The show has completed four seasons, with plans for a fifth and sixth season confirmed.

Due to the number of families and characters involved, it can be hard to keep track of the progress of each character. This guide aims to provide sufficient information on the development and story of the main characters involved in the series. Therefore, each Chapter is organized according to family.

Chapter 1: House Stark

Eddard Stark (click name for images)

Eddard Stark (The Lord of Winterfell) was one of the most powerful men in the realm, and it seemed he was on his way to greatness. He started out as one of the main characters in the series, due especially to his friendship with King Robert Baratheon, a friendship that culminated with the two men joining forces to overthrow King Aerys Targaryen (The Mad King) and leading to Robert on the iron throne.

This move was taken after Robert's love and betrothal to Ned's sister, Lyanna, who was subsequently, abducted by Prince Rhaegar, the son of King Aerys. Ned's father and brother were executed after they demanded her release from King Aerys, with The Mad King convinced that the Stark family had plans to overthrow him.

Robert kills Prince Rhaegar at the Battle of the Trident but sustains injuries in the process. Ned takes his place in command and launches an assault on the capital, Kings Landing, only to discover that House Lannister has already taken the city and murdered King Aerys and the rest of the Royal family through deceitful means. Ned is sickened by the dishonorable way in which the Lannister's have settled matters and leaves to save Lyanna, with her city under attack. However, when Ned arrives he finds his sister dying.

Ned Stark, in the beginning of the TV series, is called to King's Landing, the capital of the Seven Kingdoms, to serve as the new Hand of the King, to Robert. Initially Ned is wary of accepting the position previously held by Jon Arryn who had died suspiciously. After receiving a letter from Arryn's widow, Lysa Arryn in which she claims he was murdered, Ned accepts the role and brings his young daughters, Sansa and Arya to the capital with him.

Ned continues to explore Arryn's death and his investigations lead to him discovering that Robert's children are illegitimate. The true father of the children is Jamie Lannister, brother of Robert's wife, Cersei Lannister. Furthermore, he suspects that Arryn had been poisoned after also discovering the secret. Before Ned can tell Robert, he confronts Cersei with his discoveries and decides to be merciful, letting her gather her children and escape before the King is informed.

Cersei has other ideas though and arranges for Robert to meet his demise in a hunting accident. Before passing away, he names Ned the regent until his son, Joffrey, comes of age. Ned, knowing that Joffrey is not Robert's son and hence not eligible for the throne, contacts Robert's younger brother, Stannis, where he professes his discovery of Joffrey being illegitimate. Ned alters the will of Robert for the successor to not be Joffrey but instead, "my rightful heir".

Ned tells Littlefinger about his discoveries and rejects Littlefingers idea of allowing Joffrey to take the throne and only using the information if he proves to be a bad King. Instead, Ned asks him to arrange plans to place Cersei under arrest; however Littlefinger reveals his untrustworthiness by siding with Cersei and having the city watch kill Ned's men and arrest Ned.

The Lannister's immediately charge him with treason and Ned is forced to plead guilty in order to protect his family and be spared from death. However, at the last moment, Joffrey changes his mind, and in what is one of the most shocking moments in the series, has Ned executed, effectively triggering a war for the throne.

Catelyn Stark was the wife of Ned Stark, originally belonging to House Tully. She was the mother of

Robb Stark, Bran Stark, Arya Stark, Sansa Stark and Rickon Stark. Catelyn was well known for her kindness, generosity and was always appreciated by everyone for her honorable ways and being very protective of her family.

Peter Baelish grew up alongside Catelyn and for a long time desired her, though she was married to Ned after her betrothed, Brandon Stark, Ned's older brother, was killed by Aerys Targaryen. She may have come off as a bit rude and bossy to TV viewers, especially due to her distaste for Jon Snow, Ned's bastard son and a huge favorite amongst the audiences.

When Ned leaves Winterfell for King's Landing, Catelyn initially stays behind after their son Bran Stark is left paralyzed, thanks to Jamie Lannister who shoves him from a tower when Bran discovers the incestuous relationship between Jamie and his sister, Cersei. Catelyn thwarts an attempt on Bran's life and decides to go to the capital and inform Ned of what has happened, along with her suspicions that the Lannister's were behind it. Ned assures her that he will do everything possible to find Bran's attempted murderers. While there Baelish tells Catelyn that the knife used in the assassination attempt on her son Bran belongs to Tyrion Lannister and that he will assist her husband in exposing the truth about the attack on her son.

Catelyn sets out to return to Winterfell, only to run into Tyrion Lannister, Jamie and Cersei's brother, who Catelyn believes, tried to kill Bran. She has him forcefully taken to her sister's castle, where he is eventually released after he wins a trial by combat.

Catelyn then leaves her sisters castle, after failing to gain her support in the fight against the Lannister's, before she then meets her eldest son Robb, leading the northern armies down to face the Lannister's. Later, when she finds out about the death of her husband, she tells Robb to fight and destroy the Lannisters. She tries to get one of Robert Baratheon's brothers, Renly Baratheon to support her cause but Renly believes the crown should belong to him. While at Renley's camp she is forced to escape, along with one of his guards, Brienne of Tarth, after he is murdered by a suspicious black shadow.

When Jamie Lannister is captured in battle, she releases him and sends him with Brienne in return for the promise that Jamie will do everything in his power to ensure the safety of Arya and Sansa Stark. Vilified for releasing Jamie, she is later forgiven when Robb marries Talisa, a noblewoman from Volantis.

Catelyn is worried though about the repercussions of this marriage as Robb was sworn to marry one of Walder Frey's daughters in exchange for letting the northern armies pass through his castle. Walder Frey agrees to instead marry one of his daughters to Catelyn's brother, Edmure. However, in one of televisions most shocking events, coined "The Red Wedding" it turns out to be a setup as the wedding culminates in most of Stark's men, Robb Stark, Catelyn Stark and a pregnant Talisa Stark all being killed by the Frey's in a plot masterminded by Tywin Lannister.

The eldest son of Ned and Catelyn Stark, he was the hero who was supposed to rid the world of the Lannisters and claim the throne as his. Starting as a minor character living in his father's shadow, Robb quickly emerges as the supposed hero of the series when he first calls on and unites his banner men in the north to wage war on House Lannister, after his father is charged with treason and subsequently executed.

After Ned's execution the northern armies declare that they are now independent from the seven kingdoms and unanimously choose Robb to be the "King of the North" He quickly shows his prowess, winning several battles, with his most significant accomplishment capturing Jamie Lannister.

Later, to be given clearance to cross The Twins, an area owned by the Frey's, Robb agrees to marry one of Lord Frey's daughters. Instead, he beds and then weds Talisa, a noblewoman from Volantis who then becomes pregnant with his child.

After Lord Rickard Karstark has two young teenagers who are related to the Lannister's murdered, Robb decides to execute him. As a result of this the Karstack family withdraws their support for the King of the North and he is forced to seek support from the Frey's.

The Frey's seemingly forgive Robb for going back on his promise, when they agree to have Robbs uncle, Edmure, marry Lord Frey's daughter instead. However, after the ensuing wedding, the Freys kill most of the Stark men and Robb himself is killed by one of his own banner men, Roose Bolton.

Sansa Stark

The second eldest child of Ned and Catelyn, Sansa has been portrayed as a typical noble lady, enjoying lady like pursuits while maintaining a naïve and shallow personality, which develops throughout the series.

When King Robert visited Winterfell in the start of the series, Sansa goes on walk with her betrothed, Robert's 'son', Joffrey. An altercation between Joffrey and Arya Stark's friend led to Joffrey trying to attack Arya, who is defended by her direwolf. Sansa later denies the occurrence of any such event, which leads to her direwolf being executed at the behest of Cersei Lannister.

Sansa then leaves with Ned to King Landing, who tries to send her back to Winterfell once he realizes the truth of the relationship between Cersei and Jamie Lannister. Upset about having to leave, Sansa discloses her father's plan to Joffrey and Cersei, which ultimately ends with Ned being executed.

Sansa starts to despise Joffrey after he kills her father, but has the presence of mind to pretend to still be in love with him. She finds a companion in Ser Dontos, a knight who is saved by Sansa from being killed by Joffrey after appearing drunk.

She is nearly raped during the riots at Kings Landing, only to be saved by Sandor Clegane, who also offers to take her with him during the battle of Blackwater Bay, though she refuses.

After the Tyrells help the Lannister's in the Battle of Blackwater Bay her betrothal to Joffrey is cancelled, much to her joy, after his grandfather, Lord Tywin Lannister, decides to marry Joffrey to Margaery Tyrell. The joy is short-lived as she ends up being married to Tyrion Lannister, though the marriage is not consummated. Later, when Joffrey is killed at his wedding, Sansa is spirited off to the Vale by Lord Petyr Baelish, as she is suspected of having killed Joffrey, along with Tyrion.

While at the Vale with Lord Petyr Baelish, he informs her that he was behind the killing of Joffrey and her being able to escape. Sansa pretends to be the bastard child of Lord Baelish who is now married to Lysa Arran. Lysa informs her that she will marry her son, however later attempts to kill Sansa in a fit of jealous rage after seeing Lord Baelish kiss her. The attempt is stopped by Lord Baelish who tries to diffuse the situation before pushing Lysa through the moon door, and to her death, hundreds of feet below.

Arya Stark

One of the most beloved members of the series, Arya Stark is also one of the strongest female characters in the show, carving out her identity. She is a typical tomboy who prefers swords and archery over gowns and balls.

Arya gets into an altercation with Joffrey in Winterfell, but still travels with Ned to King's Landing later on. There, she trains with Syrio Forel, a swordsman in order to learn how to fight. Syrio gives his life for her when he holds one of the Lannister men long enough for Arya to escape.

From there, she sets off on a journey full of adventures as she goes from being a prisoner, to being a cupbearer for Tywin Lannister and later Roose Bolton. During this time she meets Jaqen H'ghar, as she releases him from being kept prisoner. As a reward he will kill three people of her choosing, to which she name's two sadistic guards and then Hagar himself. Arya agrees to unsay his name if H'ghar agrees to assist her in her escape from being a kept a prisoner at the Lannister's camp. She escapes along with Gendry and Hot Pie, before encountering H'ghar again who this time gives her a coin that will help her find him in the future.

She then joins the Brotherhood Without Banners, which she again leaves after Hot Pie and Gendry leave, before then being caught by the Hound, Sandor Clegane. The Hound decides to take her to Robb Stark in order to gain a place in his service and a reward. However, they happen upon the Stark camp just as the Red Wedding massacre, during Edmure's wedding, occurs.

The Hound then decides he will attempt to take Arya to her uncle further North in exchange for a reward. During this time the two foster an uneasy bond, and Arya grows up quickly becoming unsentimental and strong as she kills men. While they are travelling they meet Brienne of Tarth and her squire, Podrick, who are on a journey of there own to find Arya's sister, Sansa. Brienne realizes that she is Arya Stark and she and The Hound fight over who Arya should go with. Brienne wins the fight and The Hound is severly wounded.

Arya hides from Brienne and instead finds The Hound, who pleads with her to kill him. She refuses to give him a quick death and takes his money and walks away. She reaches a ship, where she shows the coin H'ghar gave her and is allowed to board.

Bran Stark

The second youngest child of Ned and Catelyn, Bran is portrayed as a determined and brave young boy who wants to become a knight.

When the Lannisters visit Winterfell, Bran spies Jamie and Cersei engaging in sexual intercourse, while he climbs the walls of his castle. Jamie, in an effort to preserve the secret of his relationship, throws Bran off the wall, which sends him into a coma and paralyzes him from waist-down. His mother and pet direwolf protect him during an assassination attempt and when he comes out of his coma, he is carried around by the fan favorite, Hodor, a giant stable boy who is only able to simply say 'Hodor'. When Robb leaves Winterfell to lead the northern armies to attack House Lannister, Bran becomes the acting Lord.

During the coma, Bran starts to have visions of a tree and a three eyed crow that informs him that he can learn how to fly. When Theon Greyjoy turns his back on the Starks and attacks Winterfell, Bran, his younger brother Rickon, wildling servant Osha and Hodor are forced to flee.

Bran's visions pave the way for his journey and he meets Jojen and Meera Reed, siblings who recognize his ability to assume the consciousness of other animals, also known as a warg. Osha is very wary of the Reed siblings and is in opposition of the plan to go the Wall, insisting they have no idea of what is beyond it. Bran insists he must go ahead and find the raven, but wants Rickon to stay safe. The group splits with just Bran, Hodor, Jojen and Meera continuing North.

Bran and his group eventually reach the giant wall and his abilities to take control and look through another's eyes are becoming stronger. Midway through their journey, they are captured by the men who took over Craster's Keep. An attack by the Night's Watch men allows them to escape and move further on their way in search for the three eyed raven. Before leaving, Bran see's his half-brother Jon Snow among the Night's Watch and motions to go towards him however Jojen holds him back, explaining that Jon will not allow him to go forth and find the raven. Bran reluctantly agrees.

The group finds the giant tree; however, before they can approach it they are attacked by Wight's, corpses reanimated by the White Walkers. During the attack Jojen is fatally wounded before they are saved by a Child of the Forest who leads them into a cave that the Wight's can not enter, due to their powers not working there.

The Child of the Forest leads them through the cave until they see the raven sitting on a throne. It then reveals itself to be a very elderly man joined with the roots of the tree. Meera exclaims that Jojen is dead but the raven explains that Jojen knew this would be his fate. The raven/elderly man explains that Jojen died so Bran could discover what he has lost. Bran inquires if this means he will help him be able to walk again, to which the raven replies no, however he will fly.

Talisa Stark

A noblewoman from Volantis, Talisa learnt medical training and left her city to tend to others. While treating a Lannister soldier injured in battle, Talisa meets Robb Stark. During their first meeting Talisa questions Robb's actions of fighting to take the Crown without having a King ready for replacement. As the story progresses, the two begin to spend more time together in between battles and start to fall in love and eventually get married, even though Robb has been promised to marry one of Lord Frey's daughters. Shortly before leaving to attend, Edmond Tully's wedding with the Frey daughter; Talisa reveals to Robb that she is pregnant with his child.

However, the marriage between Talisa and Robb is considered as a personal affront by Lord Frey and is all the motivation he needs to conspire with the Lannisters to kill the Stark men during Edmure Tully's wedding, in the Red Wedding. The massacre is initiated by one of the Freys stabbing a pregnant Talisa in the stomach, which results in the death of her as well as her baby.

Chapter 2: The Boltons

Roose Bolton

Roose Bolton, the head of House Bolton, known for torturing and flaying the skin of their dead enemies. He fought with Ned Stark during the Battle of the Trident and civil war. He is a banner man of the Starks, though ultimately reveals himself to be a cruel, vindictive man.

He answers Robb's call when Robb decides to avenge his father's death and destroy the Lannister's, though questions Robb's decision to treat the Lannister prisoners fairly. Later, he recommends his son, Ramsey, take back Winterfell as they have the Lannister's in trouble and cannot afford to turn back now.

Roose Bolton is charged with defending Harrenhal, while Robb and the rest of the forces head for Riverrun. While here, he tasks one of his subordinates, Locke, to locate and return the on-the-run Jamie Lannister, after Catelyn releases him. Jamie, minus one hand after Locke cuts it off, and Brienne are taken to Bolton at Harrenhal who agrees to release him back to his father, Tywin if he promises to inform his father that Bolton had nothing to do with his mutilation. Before Jamie leaves, Bolton tells him to send his father his regards, to which Jamie retorts to ensure he tells Robb the Lannister's send their regards, an ominous foreshadowing of events to come.

As he attends the wedding of Edmure Tully and one of Walder Frey's daughters, Bolton has secretly aligned himself with the Lannister's, and the Red Wedding is set to begin. During the celebrations, while he is seated next to Catelyn, he encourages her to look down at his wrist. She pulls his sleeve back to reveal armor and he flashes an evil smile. He himself kills Robb Stark, while telling him "the Lannister's send their regards". As a reward, the Lannister's promise him protection and he is deemed to be the Warden of the North. The day after the massacre Bolton and Frey revel in what they have done.

Bolton returns to his own lands, the Dreadnought, and discovers his bastard son Ramsey has mutilated Theon. He is frustrated with this as he feels it gives them less leverage over the Greyjoy's. He is also concerned after being told Theon didn't actually kill Bran and Rickon, with the northerners likely to back the Starks and not them should they discover this. After Ramsey takes back the Greyjoy held Moat Cailan, Bolton gives Ramsey a document legitimizing him as a Bolton.

Ramsay Snow

Ramsay is the bastard son of Roose Bolton. If there ever was a man who was crueler than Roose, it was Ramsay.

He gathers his men to take on Winterfell under Robb Stark's name. When Theon's own men betray him, Ramsay has little trouble in taking over Winterfell.

Despite assuring Theon's men that they would be shown mercy he nevertheless flays them all alive.

He then subjects Theon to brutal physical and psychological torture, which includes flaying his skin, pretending to help him escape before bringing him back, while he also cuts off Theon's genitals. Theon becomes completely subservient to Ramsey who changes his name to "Reek".

When Roose finds out what Ramsay did to Theon, he shows his anger in losing a valuable captive. However, Ramsay is able to win his father over when he shows how loyal Theon has now become and how they can use him further. Ramsey uses Theon/Reek to take back the Greyjoy held Moat Cailan and is rewarded by his father as he is given a document legitimizing him as a true son of Roose Bolton.

Chapter 3: The Lannister's

<u>Tywin Lannister</u>

There are few characters in the series that are shown to be outright evil. Tywin Lannister is one of them.

During Robert's Rebellion, Tywin used his force to destroy Aerys and had his family killed as well while sacking King's Landing.

After Catelyn captures Tyrion and takes him to the Vale, Tywin takes it as a personal affront. He despises his youngest son for resulting in the death of his wife, who died while giving birth to Tyrion, a dwarf and source of embarrassment for the House. Even though Tyrion returns, Tywin battles Robb Stark as revenge for the capture of Tyrion and is dismissive of the young northern leader's abilities.

Tywin orders his bewildered son Tyrion to lead from the front, leaving him to state his father is trying to kill him. Despite the fact that Tywin wins the battle, Robb outmaneuvers him by splitting his forces and capturing Jamie in another battle.

He is told by his advisors to offer the Starks a truce, but is impressed when Tyrion astutely states that those chances ended when Joffrey cut off Ned's head. Tywin tells his son to go to King's Landing to act as Hand of the King in his place and try to coral an increasingly sadistic and out of control Joffrey who has taken the throne. He also explicitly tells Tyrion to not bring Shae, his prostitute girlfriend with him. He defies his father's wishes though.

As well as having to deal with the attack from the north, Stannis Baratheon launches his attack on the capital. He is forced to create an alliance with the Tyrells that helps to provide the forces that bring victory to the Lannister's in the Battle of Blackwater against Stannis Baratheon.

Tywin becomes the Hand of the King again, in the hopes of running the kingdom without having to assume the position of king. He focuses on getting rid of Robb, who proves to be a greater threat than initially expected and who has got the better of his forces in three consecutive battles.

Tyrion is angry at his father for not coming to see him after he suffered injuries during the Battle of Blackwater Bay and played a huge role in devising the strategy that led to there success. Tyrion enters the room to confront his father who is seen writing a mysterious letter describing the north as "being ripe for the taking".

During the heated exchange Tywin is full of hate as he declares that despite being the heir Tyrion will never inherit Casterley Rock after he killed his mother during childbirth. As Tyrion leaves, Tywin informs him he will hang the next prostitute he finds in his room.

Tywin finally kills Robb by planning the devious Red Wedding massacre, getting rid of the Stark threat. He also decides to marry Cersei off to Ser Loras Tyrell, while marrying Tyrion to Sansa Stark. This is done in order to prevent Sansa's marriage to Loras, while making Tyrion Lord of Winterfell, as Tywin assumes that her brothers are either dead or about to die, as well as giving the Lannister's control in the North as well as the South.

During the wedding breakfast Cersei, shows who Shae is to Tywin who says that he wants her to be brought to him after the wedding. After Joffrey dies during at his wedding breakfast, his younger brother Tommen is appointed, someone Tywin believes can be controlled more easily.

After Tyrion is accused of Joffrey's murder, Tywin is named as one of the judges. The trial is filled with damning statements towards Tyrion from witnesses including his girlfriend Shea. It ends with Tyrion demanding it be resolved with a trial by combat. Tyrion's representative, Oberyn Martell is killed by Gregor Clegane and Tywin sentences his son to die.

He is then surprised by an escaping Tyrion pointing a crossbow at him while on the toilet and forced to admit he wishes his son was dead. He then dismisses Shea as a whore and warned by Tyrion not to call her that again. After repeating the word Tyrion shoots his father twice with the crossbow, killing him.

Jamie Lannister

Jamie is one of the few characters in the series who undergoes a complete personality change. He starts out as evil and arrogant, only to become seemingly selfless and compassionate.

As a member of the Kingsguard, sworn to protect the person on the iron throne, he is sometimes mocked after killing The Mad King, and is known as The

Kingslayer. The show begins with the viewer finding out about the incestuous relationship between Jamie and Cersei. Furthermore, as a member of the Kingsguard, Jamie also enjoys taking advantage of his power. His antagonism is further proven when he throws Bran off the tower in order to preserve his relationship with Cersei. He later gets into a fight with Ned, but shows some sign of fairness when he refuses to attack Ned after one of his men stabs Ned through the leg.

Jamie is then sent by Tywin to attack Robb Stark's men, where he ends up captured. After some time, he is released by Catelyn, in the company of Brienne of Tarth in order to find Sansa and Arya and send them back to her.

It is here that we witness a significant change in Jamie's personality. Even though Jamie initially goads Brienne in an attempt to get her to fight him and cut himself loose, he gets captured by a man called Locke from House Bolton who takes both Brienne and Jamie back to his camp. There, Jamie prevents Locke's men from raping Brienne by pretending that she is an heir to a fortune. However, even though his talk is able to save Brienne, Locke shows his distaste for Jamie's continued attempts to buy his favor by hacking off Jamie's right hand.

Jamie becomes delirious due to the physical and mental agony he suffers as a result from the injury, but is finally brought back to reality by Brienne. He finally starts to confide in Brienne and the viewers begin to notice a changing Jamie Lannister. He tells Brienne he broke his oath and killed the Mad King after being ordered to murder his father and burn thousands of the Kings Landing population.

Jamie is finally released when Roose Bolton arrives at the camp, but keeps Brienne. He then decides to return and saves Brienne, before returning back to King's Landing. He receives a less than euphoric welcome, with his own family making fun of the loss of his hand. The Kingslayer then sends Brienne off to look for Sansa and Arya, who have both disappeared from King's Landing, as he intends to keep his promise to Catelyn.

Jamie speaks with his father, who first gives him a sword made from Valyrian steel and then informs him that he is going to be removed from the Kingsguard and placed at Casterly Rock to rule in his place. Jamie refuses this demand, leaving his father furious and disowning him.

He has a golden hand fitted to his stump and begins to learn to fight left-handed with Bronn, with the whole experience frequently leaving him very frustrated. After Joffrey's death, he begins to grow closer to Tyrion and doubts his guilt after spending time with him while he awaits his trial.

At the trial all the witlessness give damning opinions of Tyrion. Angered at the farce and the guilty verdict that is being pushed through, Jamie see's his father during the recess and agrees to go to Casterly Rock to be the heir if Tyrion is spared death. Tywin is happy to agree to this however, Tyrion demands a trial by combat. Tyrion loses this trial and is sentenced to death. Jamie is not about to let is brother be executed though and breaks him out of his prison the night before quickly sharing an embrace as they bid each other farewell.

Cersei Lannister

A cold and ruthless woman, Cersei Lannister has been quick to get herself in the bad books of the viewers.

The viewers are quickly told about Cersei's relationship with her brother Jamie, as well as her distaste for her husband King Robert. She further antagonizes herself towards the viewership of the series when she shows no remorse over Bran being thrown down the tower by Jamie.

Other instances where Cersei has successfully drawn viewers ire include after the altercation between Arya and Joffrey, where Cersei has Sansa's direwolf killed, and when Robert dies, something later revealed to have been planned by Cersei. Afterwards, as Joffrey becomes king, Cersei tries to exert some level of influence over him without much success.

After Ned Stark confronts her with his discoveries about her and she convinces Petyr Baelish to side with her and have Ned arrested for treason. Cersei attempts further manipulation by convincing Sansa to write a letter to Robb telling him that their father will be safe if he calls off marching down to the capital and bends his knee to Joffrey. When Joffrey reneges on the promise to spare Ned if he confesses to treason, she appears to be genuinely shocked at her son's actions.

With Jamie being kept prisoner at the Stark camp, Cersei first asks Tyrion how they can get him back. He suggests the only way would be to locate Arya Stark and offer an exchange, something she tasks Lord Baelish to do. Cersi also asks her son, Joffrey for help in finding Arya, something he refuses to do. This leads to a heated argument in which Joffrey threatens to have her killed after she slaps him.

Tyrion and Cersei's relationship continues to worsen after he removes one of her trusted advisors. He jokes with her about the rumors surrounding her and

Jamie, and she responds that his greatest joke was killing their mother when he was born.

When Tyrion has her daughter Myrcella shipped off to Dorne for protection, Cersei is livid and her hatred for her brother grows with her promising him that she will one day take away someone he loves. Fearing defeat at the Battle of Blackwater she sits with her son Tommen ready to poison them both until her father triumphantly enters the room and declares they have fought off Stannis's army.

After the battle, Cersei tells Joffrey he is no longer betrothed to Sansa due the betrayal of her house, paving the way for him to marry Margeary Tyrell. However, Cersei soon starts considering Margeary a threat due to her popularity with the common folk and the ay she is easily able to manipulate people.

When Jamie returns from captivity, she is horrified by his stump and remains cold towards him well after his return. Her luck does not improve and during the

Royal Wedding, her son Joffrey is killed after being poisoned. She immediately has Tyrion arrested for the crime, even though she has no proof. After Jamie tries to convince Cersei of Tyrion's innocence, her cold rebuttal shows that their relationship has been severely damaged.

She arranges so that Tyrion's trial becomes a farce, with all the witnesses giving damning views of her brother as she seems hell-bent on having him found guilty and executed. When Oberyn Martell loses representing Tyrion in the trial of combat she smiles coldly at the result and when her father sentences him to die.

Meanwhile, she confronts her father, steadfastly refusing to go ahead with the marriage to Loris Terryl. When he dismisses her pleas, she shocks him by confirming the rumors of her and Jamie's affair. She then finds Jamie telling him she doesn't care what others think. She loves him and wants their relationship to continue, the pair then make love.

Tyrion Lannister

Probably the most popular character in the show, Tyrion is the only Lannister to be portrayed as being moral, ethical and fair while sharing the Lannister trait of possessing a high level of intelligence, something that his father and siblings also possess.

He is shown as willing to deal with Joffrey's cruelty and rudeness, slapping him several times after Joffrey refuses to offer condolences to the Starks after Bran is thrown from the tower.

He also helps Jon Snow at the Wall, when he points out that Jon Snow would benefit from befriending his comrades instead of acting superior to them. However, while returning from the Wall, he is captured by Catelyn Stark and taken to the Vale as Catelyn suspects him of attempting to murder Bran.

Tyrion manages to survive after he wins the trial by combat, when his nomination, a sellsword named Bronn, defeats Catelyn's nomination. The two develop a close kinship during the series. Tyrion leads his troops into battle against Robb Stark's men, and gets injured in the process. He also meets a prostitute name Shae, with whom he eventually falls in love.

Impressed by his son's intellectual prowess, Tywin sends Tyrion to Joffrey as Hand of the King while Tywin is away, though also warned him not to bring Shae with him, an order he disobeys. Asserting his authority he slaps Joffrey on more than one occasion when the King is getting out of hand, names Bronn as new commander of the City Watch and also arranges for Shae to be the handmaiden to Sansa. Meanwhile, his tense relationship with his sister deteriorates rapidly after he sends her daughter, Myrcella to be betrothed to the youngest son in House Martell.

Tyrion then masterminds the attack during the Battle of Blackwater by using Wildfire to destroy Stannis Baratheon's boats and rallies the army with an inspirational speech when Joffrey is taken away from the battle by Cersei. He leads the battle from the front, only to be betrayed by one of his own men but is spared death when his squire, Podrick, kills the would-be murderer.

When he awakens from his injuries, he finds he has been removed as Hand of the King and gains no recognition for his exploits in the war. He is further humiliated by his father when he asks for Casterly Rock, the Lannister stronghold. Tyrion also tries to maintain distance from Shae due to the fear that his father will kill her.

He is then made the Master of the Coin by Tywin, who also makes him wed Sansa Stark. However, Tyrion refuses to bed her until she is ready and hence, never consummates the marriage. The pair begins to bond over a common hatred for Joffrey. Despite increasing pressure from his father to get Sansa pregnant, Tyrion refuses saying he cannot, and will not do it even by force. Tywin is furious at this and reminds him of his duties as a Lannister.

One of Cersei's spies over hears an argument between Tyrion and Shae reveals the full details to the Queen. At Joffrey's and Margaery's wedding breakfast she points Shae out to her father and he states he wants to see her afterwards. Tyrion is fearful of what his father will do now that he knows who Shae is and acts cold and rudely towards her in an attempt to convince her to leave. Despite her pleas, she eventually leaves in tears.

During the wedding feast Joffrey is very rude and disrespectful towards Tyrion, forcing him to be his cup-bearer. When Joffrey dies after being poisoned, Cersei accuses Tyrion of the deed and he is then arrested. He later tells Jamie that he had no hand in the death of Joffrey, who believes him, but is unable to convince Cersei of the same.

After a string of witnesses, including Shae, give damning testimony at Tyrion's trial he finally snaps shouting towards Cersei that he couldn't be more innocent but wishes he had done it. He screams that it gave him more pleasure and relief seeing Joffrey die in such fashion than even a thousand whores. Tyrion then turns to Tywin and says the trial is a sham and he demands a trial by combat.

After Jamie and Bronn reluctantly refuse his pleas to fight for him, Oberyn Martell tells him that he will be his champion. Oberyn dominates the fight against the Mountain, Gregor Clegane; however he eventually suffers a brutal death meaning Tyrion is sentenced to die.

As he awaits his execution, Jamie surprises him by entering his cell telling him he has arranged his escape and to follow the passage way to meet Varys at a ship. The brothers share a warm embrace before Tyrion sets off to freedom. Before he does so, he decides to visit his father's bedroom. Upon entering he sees a naked women lying in the bed and is devastated to discover it is Shae. When she sees' him she grabs for the nearby knife. However, Tyrion is too quick and strangles her with Tywin's gold chain that she was wearing.

Tyrion is extremely distressed at what he has just done and apologizes to the dead body of his former lover. He picks up the crossbow and finds his father sitting on the toilet. Tywin is unable to calm his son down, infuriating him even more by referring to Shae as a whore, twice. After the second time Tyrion shoots him dead, before meeting Varys and stowing away on the ship. The bells of Kings Landing ring out, signifying the body has been found and upon hearing this Varys decides to join him on board.

Chapter 4: House Baratheon

Robert Baratheon

Strong, powerful and not the most intelligent person, King Robert Baratheon enjoyed winning the kingdom more than the actual process of running it. After his love, Lyanna Stark, was abducted and possibly raped by Prince Rhaegar, son of King Aerys II, who also killed Ned's father and brother, Robert and Ned fought together to destroy King Aerys and took over the kingdom.

The show starts with Robert making his way to Winterfell, where he asks Ned to be the Hand of the King in order to run the kingdom giving Robert more time to enjoy his pursuits; drinking, eating and having sex. He also offers to marry Joffrey to Sansa. After Robert returns to King's Landing, he orders the death of Daenerys and Viserys Targaryen, children of Aerys II, as he is afraid they may attempt to fight him for the kingdom. Ned resigns in protest of the decision, but is reinstated later. His wife, Cersei, hates him but insists she loved him when they were first married. Robert though states he could never love her in return due to his feelings for Lyanna.

After reinstating Ned, Robert goes on a hunt, where he gets seriously injured. Robert makes Ned the Protector of the Realm before finally succumbing to his injuries, never even finding out that his children were never really his own.

Stannis Baratheon

Stannis is the younger brother of King Robert Baratheon and is known for his strict sense of justice and an otherwise boring personality. One of his most loyal men includes Davos Seaworth, who is one the few people Stannis respects.

After Robert dies, Stannis is revealed as the rightful heir to the throne due to Robert's children being illegitimate. To support this claim he sends copies to High Lords across the seven kingdoms of the letter Ned Stark sent to him revealing Cersei and Jamie's relationship. However, the Lannister's proclaim Joffrey to be the rightful heir and do not entertain Stannis's claim.

Meanwhile, Stannis falls under the spell of his priestess, Melisandre, who deems that the Lord of the Light has foreseen that Stannis will emerge as king. Refusing to align with both, his brother Renly, and Robb Stark, Stannis manages to quickly alienate himself from the rest of the realm while the influence of Melisandre grows. Melisandre then births a dark Shadow in front of Davos Seaworth, which then kills Renly and allows Stannis to take over Renly's troops.

Stannis then attempts to take over King's Landing, with the plan culminating in the Battle of Blackwater. Despite the Lannister's using Wildfire to set ablaze many of the ships before they reach the shore, many troops still do, including Stannis himself who is leading the charge. It appears as if he will be victorious until Tywin Lannister leads his and House Tyrells troops into the battle and he is forced to withdraw.

The loss shakes his belief in Melisandre, though she is able to restore it later when showing him a vision in the flames. Davos returns after being rescued by a pirate, but is met with a cold and withdrawn Stannis. Davos is convinced that Melisandre has brain washed him and tries to kill her, an act that see's him thrown in jail.

Melisandre leaves to go and find some King's blood, and returns with Gendry, one of King Roberts many bastard children, with intentions of sacrificing him. Stannis visits Davos in jail and the latter pleads for him to release Gendry, stating he has done nothing wrong and doesn't deserve this. Stannis dismisses this but Davos reasons that the real reason he came to see him was because he knew deep in his heart that it was wrong and Davos would tell him so. After Davos gives his word that Melisandre will not be attacked again he is released.

Stannis credits Melisandre for the death of Joffrey and Robb, as she says she prayed to the Lord of the Light for their deaths. After Davos secretly releases Gendry, Stannis accuses him of betrayal and sentences him to death. However, he relents after Davos shows him a letter from the Nights Watch asking for help against the White Walkers. After the Iron Bank of Braavos provide a loan, Stannis takes his army north of the Wall after Davos and Melisandre both convince him to fight against the real threat, which is the White Walkers.

Renly Baratheon

The youngest brother of Robert and Stannis Baratheon, Renly is a closeted homosexual whose inviting personality endears him to his men.

The audience is first introduced to Renly when he greets Ned on his arrival at King's Landing. He is also shown to have a not-so-secret relationship with Ser Loras Tyrell. Even though Loras tries to convince Renly to take the throne if Robert dies, Renly dismissed the idea. However, when Robert gets injured, Renly suggests to Ned that they should kidnap Joffrey and let Renly take the thrones, which Ned dismisses as treason. After the disagreement, Renly flees the city.

Renly makes a claim to the throne by marrying Loras's sister, Margeary Tyrell, and gaining 100,000 men to take over the throne. He then blocks off supply from the High Gardens of the Tyrell family in order to create a famine situation in King's Landing.

In a tournament hosted by Renly, Loras is defeated by a woman, Brienne of Tarth, who is then admitted into his Kingsguard.

Renly goes to meet Stannis, with the latter offering his younger brother a position on the small council and to be his heir if he supports him. Later, Catelyn visits Renly in order to convince him to join Robb's cause, but is refused. While she is alone with Brienne and Renly in his command tent, the Shadow that was birthed by Melisandre swoops in and kills Renly by stabbing him through the chest. With his death, the Tyrell troops return to Highgarden and Renly's change allegiances to Stannis.

Joffrey Baratheon

It would be more appropriate to call him Joffrey
Lannister, as he is actually the son of Jamie and
Cersei Lannister, and not Robert Baratheon. He is
easily one of the cruelest and most sadistic characters
to appear on television.

Joffrey gets betrothed to Sansa Stark during his
family's visit to Winterfell, but things quickly go awry
when he gets in a fight with Arya's friend and is then
attacked by Arya and her direwolf. After Robert dies,
Joffrey becomes king, even though he is not a true
heir of Robert. He gets Ned, who had openly claimed
that Joffrey was a result of Cersei and Jamie's
relationship, to accept charges as treason. Ned agrees
only to still be beheaded after Joffrey changes his
mind, effectively starting the War of the Five Kings.

As time passes his reign becomes even more about
sadism and cruelty. He orders the tongue of a singer
to be ripped out after he displeases him, forces a

whore to beat the other viciously, and shoots an arrow through another. When he confronts his mother after hearing rumors surrounding his parentage, the argument leads to her slapping him and him reacting by threatening her with death and ordering every single one if his father's bastard children to be executed.

He particularly seems to enjoy being unpleasant to Sansa. Joffrey takes her to the place where her father's head has been impaled on a spike and forces her to look at it. He forces her to strip and beats her after her brother Robb wins an important battle. He even orders Robb's decapitated head to be brought to Kings Landing so he can serve it to her at his wedding feast, though thankfully for her sake Tyrion steps in.

As time passes Joffrey begins to lose popularity amongst the common folk, many of whom detest him as they are struggling to survive. After he is among those who see off his sister, who is being sent to live with the House Martell, a riot breaks out when cow dung is splatted across his face. Joffrey orders his guards to kill everybody in sight, and chaos erupts. Joffrey manages to escape back to safety only to be confronted by a furious Tyrion who admonishes him for being a malicious fool.

At the Battle of Blackwater, Joffrey is full of bravado after seeing the destruction that his uncle's has caused with the wildfire. However, this quickly dissipates when he realizes that there are still a large number of Stannis' forces reaching the shore. When his troops seem to be losing and the battle begins turning Joffrey happily returns to his mother on her orders. This cowardice lowers his men's morale. Luckily for him they still emerge victorious after Tywin intercedes on their behalf bringing extra forces, both Lannister and Tyrell. He then breaks of his impending marriage with Sansa and decides to marry Margeary Tyrell instead.

Joffrey continues making inhumane decisions much to the chagrin of his grandfather and mother. His impending marriage to Margaery does wonders for his popularity though, as she is loved by the people. On one occasion she convinces him to open the doors while they are visiting the location of their upcoming wedding and they are met with joyous applause. Cersei, is not as impressed as she feels that Margeary is simply manipulating her son.

Joffrey marries Margeary and during his wedding feast, is behaving particularly immaturely and spitefully, especially to Tyrion, who he orders to be his cup-bearer. He sips from his cup only to begin choking and vomiting with his face turning purple and blood dripping out of his eyes and nose. With his last act of strength he raises his finger towards Tyrion who is immediately placed under arrest and charged with Regicide.

It is later revealed that Petyr Baelish and Olenna Tyrell conspired to poison and kill Joffrey. Olenna, Margaery's grandmother, informs her she played a part in the murder in order to protect her after seeing the way he had acted towards Sansa.

Chapter 5: Camp Stannis

Ser Davos Seaworth

Ser Davos Seaworth is a former pirate, who endeared himself to Stannis Baratheon, after providing a trapped and starving Stannis with smuggled onions during Robert's Rebellion. Stannis rewards him with a knighthood and land, however, as he is a former smuggler, Stannis cut off four of his fingers as a punishment for these crimes.

Davos maintains his distrust of Melisandre, the priestess who seems to have cast a spell on Stannis, but does not directly interfere. Davos also tries to convince Stannis to align with Renly and fight Joffrey, but Stannis refuses to consider this possibility. He helps take Melisandre to the cave under Renly's camp where he watches in shock and horror she gives birth to a dark shadow, responsible assassinates Renly.

Davos then recruits a pirate, Salladhor Saan, to help Stannis during the Battle of Blackwater, which still results in defeat for Stannis and the death of Davos' son after the wildfire explosion obliterates his ship killing him and sending Davos crashing overboard.

Davos is is rescued from the sea by the pirate whom he convinced to join the battle, Salladhor. He returns to Stannis, after learning that Melisandre is setting light to anyone who questions her. He threatens to kill her but is quickly arrested and jailed by Stannis. However, he is soon released on the condition that he will not attempt to strike Melisandre ever again.

Davos further antagonizes himself to Stannis when he releases Gendry, Robert's bastard whose blood and sacrifice Melisandre needed in order to ensure victory for Stannis. He averts his sentence of death when he presents a letter he received from the Nights Watch pleading for help against the White Walkers. Davos and Melisandre convince Stannis they are the real threat and they head past the Wall.

Melisandre

A priestess who seems to have bound Stannis in her spell, Melisandre is as devious as she is beautiful.

Often referred to as The Red Women, her ceremonies for the God of Light are not appreciated by either Davos or Maester Cressen, but Stannis refuses to hear a word against her and he and the vast majority his household follow the religion blindly.

Melisandre is instrumental in convincing Stannis to not seek an alliance with anyone else as the Lord of the Light is with him. When Cressen tries to poison Melisandre with wine, he drinks it first to fool the priestess in believing that it wasn't poisoned. Melisandre realized his ruse and drank anyway, but remained perfectly healthy while Cressen immediately died.

Melisandre then has Davos take her to a cave, where she gives birth to a dark Shadow, which enters Renly's private tent and kills him there, giving Stannis command of his dead brother's men. However, at the behest of Davos, Stannis does not take Melisandre to the Battle of Blackwater, where he suffers a severe defeat. When he returns, he criticizes Melisandre and doubts whether she can help him win. He begins strangling her furiously and regrets murdering his brother. However, she soon placates him by reminding him of the magic they have already created and that he will commit far worse acts of betrayal. She shows him an image in the fire, which helps renew his faith in the priestess.

After the defeat at Blackwater Bay, Stannis isolates himself from everyone except Melisandre. While Stannis is withdrawn and recovering from the defeat, she uses the time to burn more non-believers alive in the name of the Lord of Light.

Melisandre then finds the Brotherhood Without Banners, where she has Gendry taken and brought back. She uses Gendry to extract his blood, which is necessary for her plans to bring Stannis to power. She plans to execute him after she takes the blood, but Davos sets him free before that can happen. However, she convinces Stannis not to execute Davos for his treason as the Lord of the Light had deemed the pirate to be integral in their future plans. Davos presents the letter he received outlining the threat of the White Walkers beyond the Wall and Melisandre agrees, helping to convince Stannis this is where they should be focusing their attentions. When she, Stannis and his army arrive past the Wall she seems to pay particularly close attention to Jon Snow.

Chapter 6: The Night's Watch

Jon Snow

The bastard son of Ned, Jon Snow has proven to be another fan favorite, displaying his fighting prowess and bravery on numerous occasions. Catelyn is particularly resentful of his presence at Winterfell, though cared for him when he was sick as a child. Jon is also very close with his half-sibling's Robb and Arya.

When Jon finds out he can't go to King's Landing with Ned, he decides to join the Night's Watch, which he initially dislikes as his dreams of defending the lands from White Walkers and Wildlings are somewhat different from what he see's when he arrives, a place for criminals to be dumped. Later he becomes friends with his fellow comrades after he impresses them with his excellent fighting skills.

When he swears his oath and officially joins he is disappointed to only be named a steward instead of a ranger. He wrongly assumes it's due to tension between him and Ser Alliser Thorne; however, the Lord Commander Jeor Mormont wants him to work under him, with the inference that he maybe grooming him to take charge in the future.

When Jon learns of his father's execution he immediately leaves to join Robb and his forces only to be convinced to turn around by Samwell Tarly and others. Mormont tells him that they are planning to go beyond the Wall in numbers to find out more about the threat posed. Jon assures him he will not desert again.

Jon joins the Night's Watch beyond the Wall, and they split up into smaller scouting parties with Jon chosen to be in Qhorin's group. His group ambushes some Wildlings though when Jon see's that the person in front of him is a woman, called Ygritte, he is hesitant to kill her. The hesitancy gets him separated from the rest of his group and he ties her up and looks for them. Unable to find them, Ygritte eventually manages to escape and leads him into an ambush this time, from the Wildlings.

When Jon is taken to one of their camps and sees' Qhorin, also being held captive, and who reveals that the rest of their scouting group are dead after looking for him. He tells Jon to ensure that they died for a good cause and that he should become a spy in the Wildlings camp by presenting him as a traitor to the Night's Watch. Qhorin immediately begins taunting and insulting Jon until they eventually fight, where Jon stabs him, leaving the Wildlings impressed and shocked. Before he dies his senior whispers to him a line from the Night's Watch oath.

Jon is taken to see the Wildlings leader, Mance Raider, and convinces him of his intentions to leave the Night's watch and join the Wildlings. Mance explains his reasons for gathering all the Wildlings together, to escape from the White Walkers and take over the seven kingdoms, and they come across the devastating attack the White Walkers and Wight's unleashed on the Night's Watch.

During his tenure with the wildlings, he falls in love with Ygritte. The pair, along with several others, scales the giant Wall along with some of the wildlings, though Jon turns on them after refusing to kill an old man and joins the Night's Watch again.

After recovering from injuries sustained during his escape from the Wildlings Jon is forced to stand before a panel of the Night's Watch. Jon admits to killing Qhorin, having sex and being with wildlings. He also tells them of Mace Raider's plans and after deliberation is spared death.

Jon convinces them that they must deal with the mutineers who have take over Craster's Keep; as if Mance get's a hold of them he will learn of the

Watch's depleted forces. Jon and his fellow brothers kill the rebels, rescue Crasters many, many wives and unwittingly save his step-brother Bran.

The Night's Watch then begins to make plans for Mance Raider's impending invasion. Waking to the sound of a great horn, Jon looks out a top of the Wall and see's a huge ball of flames, signifying Mance and his army has arrived. Meanwhile, another horn blows horning of the danger as Tormond, Ygritte and others are approaching from another direction.

Suffering many casualties the Night's Watch just about survive the night; though manage to inflict many deaths on the other side. Among those dead is his lover Ygritte who dies in his arms. The following morning as they survey the death and destruction Jon tells Sam of his plan to put an end to the invasion, he is going to kill Mance Raider and plunge the Wildlings into chaos without the only thing bringing all the disparate groups together.

Seemingly on a suicide mission, Jon makes his way to the Wildlings camp and demands an audience with Mance to open negotiations. Mance however, realizes Jon's true intentions when he notices him glancing at a sharp knife. They are interrupted though by the sound of horns and Stannis' army arriving to kill copious amounts of Wildlings. As they burn the Wildlings dead bodies to prevent them turning into Wight's, Jon looks through the fire to see Melisandre retuning his gaze.

Samwell Tarly

Timid and easily scared, few would have felt safe with Samwell Tarly defending the Wall. However, he made up for these flaws with unwavering loyalty and occasions of extreme bravery.

Sam arrives at Castle Black of the Night's Watch only to be ridiculed because of his weight and timidity. He finds a companion in Jon Snow, who defends him from the bullies and they develop a close friendship.

Sam soon proves his intelligence to the Lord Commander, Jeor Mormont, and displays his loyalty by running after Jon Snow to convince him to return after Jon abandons the Night's Watch when he hears of his father's execution.

Sam is part of the group that goes beyond the Wall with the Lord Commander, where they cross Caster's Keep, the house of a wildling who marries his daughters and seems to not have any sons, sacrifices it is later revealed for the White Walkers. There, he meets one of Craster's daughters, Gilly, with whom he slowly falls in love.

While Sam collects dung for fuel with some of his comrades, three horns blasts are heard, which signal the arrival of White Walkers. Even though the others run away, Sam is too slow to escape the Walkers. However, he hides behind a rock and is able to save himself until one finally notices him. Thankfully, Sam is ignored for some reason and hence, survives.

After the attack, and with dwindling numbers, Mormont is angry with him for not sending any ravens to warn the Seven Kingdoms of the attack. Additionally, some of the others want to leave him behind due to him hiding during the fight and generally slowing them down.

The group retreats to Craster's Keep, where Gilly gives birth to Craster's son. Meanwhile, some men of the Night's Watch turn on the Lord Commander and his men, killing Jeor and the men who remained loyal to the Night's Watch. Sam escapes with Gilly. When a White Walker attacks them in the night, wanting her child, Sam kills it with the Dragonglass he found.

He finally makes it back to Castle Black, where he is told to write letter to warn Westeros of the impending arrival of White Walkers. He is also present to meet Jon after Jon escapes from the wildlings and returns.

Sam, who is mockingly called "the slayer" after his claims of killing a White Walker, takes Gilly to Mole's Town in order to protect, though later learns it has been sacked by the Wildlings. That sadness turns to joy when he hears her voice banging on the gate pleading to be let in after surviving the attack in Moles Town.

During the assault by Mance, Sam tells Gilly to stay in a storage room and the two kiss before he leaves. Sam shows bravery during the battle, surviving various attacks and managing to release Jon's direwolf, Ghost, to help them. When Jon tells Sam of his plan to kill Mance Raider he pleads with him not to go but fails. The friends say goodbye before Jon sets off.

Ser Jeor Mormont

Lord Commander of the Night's Watch, Jeor Mormont left the comfort of his home to join the Night's Watch.

During a visit from Tyrion Lannister, Jeor asks him to relay t the King and Queen that are in great need of more resources. He makes Jon Snow his steward, who resents the job before realizing that Jeor simply wants to train him in order to become Lord Commander one day. Later, Jon saves Jeor's life by killing a White Walker in the commander's room by setting it on fire. He gives Jon a sword made from Valyrian steel as a reward. When Jon deserts he does not punish him, he instead states that the far bigger threat is beyond the Wall and not the battle for the throne.

Realizing the threat of the Walkers, Jeor organizes a group who go beyond the Wall, where they seek refuge at Craster's Keep. After leaving Craster's Keep, the men are faced with the arrival of the White

Walkers, forcing them to retreat to Craster's Keep. During this attack Jeor saves Samwell Tarly from being killed by a Wight, but is furious when he learns Sam didn't release ravens asking for help.

Jeor and the remaining bedraggled and exhausted troops arrive at Craster's Keep. Craster is an unsympathetic host though, taunting and haranguing the troops. He says that Jeor and his men have recovered enough and should kill any of those still recovering. After a heated exchange when some of the Night's Watch complaining of the food and conditions, Craster orders them all to leave. Despite Jeor attempting to control the situation, the troops have had enough and, one of them, Rast kills Craster and punches one of his wives, then threatens her with a knife, demanding to know where the food is kept.

Jeor is apoplectic, curses his troops for their actions and draws his sword towards the man holding the knife. While the two square off, Rast stabs Jeor in the back, Jeor drops his weapon and finds the strength to turn around and begin strangling Rast. Chaos and death ensue as those remaining loyal to Jeor Mormont fight with mutineers. Jeor continues clasp Rast by the throat but the initial knife wound has done too much damage and starts to cough up blood and falling down. Rast seizes the initiative kills Jeor, repeatedly stabbing him in the throat.

His skull is used as a cup to drink wine from by the mutineers who abuse the women drink until Jon Snow and the rest of the Night's Watch come to kill them.

Chapter 7: Across the Narrow Sea

Daenerys Targaryen

Initially coming across as meek and timid, Daenerys soon becomes a fearless *khaleesi* commanding the respect of those around her.

The daughter of King Aerys II, Daenerys is initially married off to the Dothraki's Khal Drogo, by her brother Viserys. He does this in an attempt to gain 40,000 of Drogo's men, which he intends to use to take over the Iron Throne. At her wedding to Drogo she is given three solid dragon eggs as a gift before being taken away by Drogo on a white horse. She initially does not want to either marry or engage in sexual intercourse with Drogo, but with time she falls in love with him.

She uses the advice of one of her servants to utilize her sexuality and gain confidence around Drogo and soon gets pregnant with Drogo's son. Viserys, though grows angry over not receiving the men he was promised, and jealous of his sister's increasing power. He becomes violent and threatens Daenerys. Viserys arrives drunk at a feast and draws his sword on Drago and demands his army, threatening Daenerys again. Drogo has had enough and kills him by pouring molten gold on his head.

Soon after King Robert launches an assassination attempt on Daenerys to kill her and her unborn child via poising though she is saved before she can drink it by her trusted advisor Ser Jorah Mormont. In retaliation for this, Drogo decides to lead his army to attack King's Landing.

Before they can even pan the attack though, Drogo is challenged to a duel by one of his men who disapprove of Daenerys's interventions in the actions of the khalasar after she objects to the treatment of the women in a town that they sack. Even though Drogo win's the battle easily, he sustains a wound which becomes infected, leading to his death and most of the khalasar abandoning her.

Daenerys gives birth but the child is stillborn. However, she becomes the Mother of Dragons when she steps into the blaze started for Drogo's cremation, along with the three dragon eggs she was given earlier on, and emerges unscathed with three baby dragons. The remaining Dothraki members bow down and proclaim her their Queen.

She leads her exhausted group to the city of Qarth. Seeing herself as mother to three dragons, she teaches them to breathe fire on command. Xaro, one of the Thirteen that rule the city offers to fund her invasion of Kings Landing if she accepts his marriage proposal.

Daenerys fails to win support from the group of Thirteen and returns to find her guards have been killed and her dragons have been stolen. Xaro arranges a meeting of the Thirteen so she can appeal to them for help. At the meeting, Pyat Pree a warlock declares he is responsible and Xaro states he is taking control of the city before the warlock kills the other members in the room using his magic. Pyat invites her to come and get her dragons and Daenerys escapes.

Daenerys visits the House of the Undead, home to Pyat, and overcomes many tricks and illusions before becoming trapped. Pyat appears and tells her that she and her dragons are now his prisoners. However, she instructs her dragons to breathe fire using the command she taught them and they burn him alive. Determined to confront Xaro for his treachery she discovers him in bed with a trusted advisor she thought to be dead. Daenerys orders them to inside Xaro's vault, which turns out to be empty, and locks them inside to die.

She then makes her way to Slaver's Bay, where she purchases all the unsullied warriors (eunuchs who are trained in the art of fighting from a young age) and kills all the slave masters in the city of Astopor. She gives all the slaves their freedom, but they all are decide to fight for her. Ser Barriston Selmy, relived of his duties by Joffrey, saves her from being assassinated again when he reveals himself. He joins her Queensguard as another experienced advisor.

She also gains the services of **Daario Naharis** a captain, of the second sons (a sell sword company) who seems intrigued by Daenerys and who kills his partners when they decide to murder Daenerys. Dario proves himself to be an excellent soldier and proves vital to taking control of Yunkai. The people of Yunkai lift her up and celebrate their freedom.

Her dragons are getting increasingly bigger, more violent and she is struggling to control them. She then moves to Meereen where she again frees the cities slaves and has many of the slave owners murdered and placed on crosses, similar to what Daenerys saw they had done previously to slave children as she approached the city.

She receives word that after leaving, Yunkai has re-established slavery and Astapor, the council she instructed to be set has been taken over by a butcher. In response to this she puts aside any ideas of invading the Seven Kingdoms in the near future to learn how to rule here first.

Daenerys banishes Ser Jorah after learning he was acting as a spy for Varys before sitting down in the throne room to hear from the day's supplicants. A shepherd enters carrying something in a blanket. He opens it up to reveal burnt bones and says his three-year old daughter was burnt to death by a winged shadow. Daenerys realizes it was one of her dragons and that she cannot control the risk that they pose anymore. She chains two of them up in the catacombs, the third cannot be found, and closes the stone door, leaving them inside.

Khal Drogo

Drogo is a warrior and the leader, or khalasar of the Dothraki, a group of savage, fierce warriors who are very skilled in fighting.

Drogo is offered the hand of Daenerys if he provides Viserys with 40,000 men to which he agrees. When Viserys sees Drogo he comments on the length of his hair and is told that Dothraki will only cut it when they are defeated, suggesting he is a fearsome and highly-skilled warrior. Even though Daenerys is initially afraid of Drogo, she eventually falls in love with him and Drogo is happy with her as his wife and when she informs him that she is with child. When Viserys continues to act violent and threaten Daenerys, including cutting her open and leaving Drogo the child, Drogo has had enough and kills him by pouring molten gold over his head.

Daenerys asks him to cross the sea and carry out the invasion, however, he says his people are wary of ships and the sea as they don't trust water their horses cannot drink. This feeling changes though when Daenerys survives an assassination attempt, ordered by King Robert. Drogo vows to have his revenge and take over the Seven Kingdoms.

To help pay for the invasion, Drago leads the Dothraki to ransack a village in order to round up slaves they can trade for ships. Daenerys orders the troops to stop with their violent treatment against women and although he says it is Dothraki custom, sides with his Khaleesi. Some of the Dothraki are enraged and he is challenged by one of his men over Daenerys' increasing power. In the ensuing battle, Drogo wins but suffers a wound, which later gets infected.

Drago's condition continues to worsen and he falls from his horse, something considered an embarrassment for the Dothraki as he is seen as being unfit to lead. A desperate Daenerys turns to one of the woman that she saved and who happens to be a witch. She pleads with her to uses magic to ensure he lives but the Dothraki are agitated over the use of witchcraft and in the ensuing argument Daenerys is pushed to the ground causing her to go into labor.

Her child is stillborn and disfigured, and Drogo is left in a catatonic state. The witch says she did this on purpose as retaliation for sacking her village. Realizing that she has lost her husband, Daenerys kills him by suffocating him with a pillow. The witch is tied to Drago's funeral pyre and burned alive.

Ser Jorah Mormont

Ser Jorah left Westeros in disgrace after selling poachers to slavery in order to pay off his debts. He is sent by Varys to spy on Daenerys, but he later comes to respect her and falls in love with her as well.

Jorah takes good care of Daenerys, willing to do anything for her. Initially he tries to keep Viserys under control, but meets with little success in this regard. He does prevent an assassination attempt on Daenerys that was ordered by King Robert.

When Drogo dies, Jorah tries to convince Daenerys not to climb into his burning pyre. When Daenerys emerges unscathed, Jorah immediately proclaims his loyalty to her. When the Khalasar enters the city of Qarth, Jorah confesses that he is attracted to Daenerys, who does not reciprocate the feelings. While in Qarth he also assists her in recovering the three dragons from Pyat Pree.

Jorah continues providing advice to Daenerys, who acts on the advice only if she agrees with it. He is instrumental in helping Daenerys free the cities of Astopor, Yunkai and Mereen. When Daenerys shows signs of being attracted to Daario Naharis, Jorah is noticeably unhappy.

Barristan Selmy informs Daenerys that Jorah has been spying on her the whole time for Varys who was informing Robert Baratheon back in Kings Landing. She is particularly upset when he admits that he told of her pregnancy and how it led to the assassination attempt on her being ordered by Robert. She orders him to leave immediately, giving him one day and leaving him of no uncertainty of his fate if he disobeys. She tells him that if he sill remains in Meereen after that than his head will be thrown in the sea. Later, Jorah is seen riding away from the city.

Viserys Targaryen

The son of King Aerys II and the brother of Daenerys Targaryen, Viserys is a spiteful and whining man who would do anything to get an army to take over Westeros; even sell off his sister.

Yes, in the start of the series, Viserys marries off Daenerys Targaryen to Khal Drogo in exchange of the promise of 40,000 men that will help him take over Westeros. So obsessed with the Iron Throne is Viserys, he tells Daenerys he will let every Dothraki rape her if it means he is King.

Viserys travels with the khalasar until he receives the men he has been promised, only to grow more irate as time passes and he gets nothing. After seeing how Daenerys is becoming more powerful and influential over the Dothraki, he tries to steal the three dragon eggs given to his sister on her wedding day, only for Ser Jorah to stop him.

After threatening Daenerys and her unborn baby in front of the Khalasar and Khal Drogo, Drogo finally tires of Viserys and kills him by pouring molten gold over his head.

Chapter 8: The Wildlings

Mance Ryder

The leader of the wildlings, Mance Ryder manages to unify the 100 different tribes under him and has plans to attack and take over the Night's Watch.

When Craster informs the Night's Watch of Mance's plans to attack them, Lord Commander Jeor Mormont sends out a group of men, including Jon Snow to find out the threat. However, Jon Snow ends up being captured by a wildling, Ygritte, and is taken to Mance Ryder. However, in an effort to prove that Jon wants to join the wildlings, he kills a feared member of the Night's Watch; Qhorin Halfhands (remember it was Qhorin's idea for Jon to kill him and gain the trust of the wildlings.)

During Mance's first meeting with Jon he asks the Night's Watch member how he thinks he has managed to unite all the different tribes. When Jon replies he doesn't know, Mance informs him he simply told them they would die if they don't go south, in reference to the scale of the threat posed by the White Walkers.

Mance see's the carnage the White Walkers have inflicted on the Night's Watch and he orders a small group to climb the Wall, including Jon, Ygritte and Mance's second-in-command, Tormund Giantsbane. Mance tells them to wait on the other side of the Wall for the signal to attack, which he reveals will be the biggest fire the north has ever seen.

Jon comes to negotiate with Mance after the battle between the Wildlings and Night's Watch. Mance tells him his aim is not to defeat the Nights Watch but to be on the other side when the White Walkers arrive. Jon glances at a nearby knife and Mance understands why he is really there.

Before anything happens they hear the horns from Stannis' army who arrive and slaughter many Wildlings. Mance refuses to bow down to Stannis but Jon convinces Stannis to not execute Mance, after remembering how he spared hi own life previously. Stannis, out of respect for Jon's father shows mercy, agreeing to have him arrested instead.

Tormund Giantsbane

Tormund Giantsbane is a skilled fighter who is the second-in-command to the King-Beyond-the-Wall, Mance Ryder.

Jon Snow initially perceives Tormund to be the King-Beyond-the-Wall, before being corrected by Mance Ryder. Tormund is accompanied by Jon, Ygritte and around twenty other wildlings as they make their way to climb the Wall. Tormund is forced to accept Jon's word that he has abandoned the Night's Watch, but still harbors his reservations on Jon's honesty.

Tormund climbs down the Wall and starts making his way towards Castle Black, where he orders Jon to kill a man, who does not follow the order. Tormund decides to kill Jon as he realizes he cannot be trusted, but Jon manages to kill several of Tormund's men before escaping.

Tormund leads the assault on the Castle Black while Mance Raider is attacking from the other side of the wall. Tormund kills several members of the Night's Watch and engages in an evenly contested fight with Ser Allinson Thorne before wounding him. Eventually, he is the only one of those leading the rear assault left until Jon Snow incapacitates him with a crossbow. He is taken for interrogation and visited by Jon Snow after Stannis's army arrives to defeat the Wildlings. He tells Jon that Ygritte loved him, and her talk of killing him proof of it. He asks if Jon will burn her body north of the Wall as she would have wanted a request Jon agrees to.

Ygritte

As beautiful as she is intelligent, Ygritte is a wildling who becomes the love interest of Jon Snow.

She is initially captured by Jon, who refuses to kill her. This hesitation allows Ygritte to escape, before being captured by Jon again. She teases him over his Night's Watch vows, to not have sex and she manages to escapes again. However this time when Jon follows her, he is captured by wildlings. Jon then kills Qhorin Halfhand, a fellow member of the Night's Watch, to convince the wildlings that he stands for their cause, and is accepted by their leader, Mance Ryder.

After they the Wildlings come across the wreckage left by the White Walkers attack on the Nights Watch, Ygritte playfully lures Jon into a cave. She begins undressing with the intention of ensuring he has forgotten his vows and the pair have sex. Afterwards, Ygritte wishes they never had to leave the cave. Ygritte is part of the group that Mance sends to climb the wall, and nearly falls to her death only to be saved by Jon. They reach the top and share a passionate kiss.

After Jon betrays the wildlings and flees, he is found by Ygritte again. Even though he tells her that he loves her and she clearly does too, she is stung by his treachery and shoots him three times with her bows, but is unable to kill him. She watches tearfully as he manages to flee on is horse. While resting at camp with Tormund he comments to her that she must really love Jon as he would be dead otherwise.

Later, she is seen with Tormund, still angry at Jon for his betrayal, waiting for the signal by Mance Ryder. She participates in the attack on Mole Town and spares the lives of Gilly and her son when she discovers them, even motioning for them to remain quiet to avoid detection.

Ygritte is part of the attack on Castle Black and kills several of the Nights Watch before she comes across

Jon again. Pointing her bow at him, the two stare at each other, neither one able to move and her determination to kill weakens. However, a young boy of the Night's Watch shoots an arrow through her back and she dies as Jon cradles her. A devastated Jon burn's her body north of the Wall as Tormund explains it's what she would have wanted.

Gilly

Gilly is the daughter as well as wife of Craster, a wildling who, as the viewers can easily guess, marries his daughters.

When the Night's Watch camps at Craster's Keep, Gilly asks Sam to take her away from the place, but Jon Snow refuses as he cannot risk Craster's alliance. Sam promises to return one day and take her away, giving her a thimble, his only remaining possession from his mother.

After the White Walkers attack the Night's Watch, the survivors retreat to Craster's Keep, where Gilly gives birth to Craster's son. Gilly worries about saving her son from Craster because she knows that Craster sacrifices the male babies to the White Walkers.

When some of the men from the Night's Watch rebel and kill Craster, Lord Jeor Mormont and other the loyal members, Sam and Gilly run away, even killing a White Walker in the process. They manage to make it back to Castle Black and become ever closer along the way. They reach the sanctuary of Castle Black where she is provided with refuge.

Gilly assists in the kitchen but Sam remains fearful of her safety due to many recruits for the Night's Watch being violent criminals. Despite her protesting about being kept apart from him he takes her to Moles Town for safety. Ironically though, the Wildlings soon attack there and she and her baby are only spared by Ygritte discovering them and urging them to remain quiet.

After the attack, Gilly makes her way back to Castle Black and Sam is ecstatic to see her after fearing she had been killed. Later, during as the Night's Watch prepares to fight Mance's army, Sam hides her in a storage room and she pleads with him to stay with her. He promises her that he won't die and the two kiss. After the battle, Sam returns and the pair are reunited.

Chapter 9: Other Major Characters

<u>Varys</u>

Varys is a eunuch who is also the Master of Whispers. He is as sneaky a character as any in the series, making full use of his informants all across the lands.

Varys is part of the small council that sits in King's Landing. When Robert dies, he tries to dissuade Ned from supporting Stannis's claim, but fails to receive a favorable response. When Ned is in the dungeon Varys comes to visit him and is unimpressed that he trusted Petyr Baelish over him and how he told Cersei he knew about Joffrey

Varys tries to intervene and negotiate the release of Ned by convincing Ned it's in his best interests to acknowledge Joffrey as King. This endeavor ultimately fails though when Joffrey orders the execution of Ned Stark to still take place.

Later, Varys finds out about Tyrion's prostitute and lover, Shae, but promises to keep it a secret and even installs Shae as Sansa Stark's hand maiden. He and Tyrion develop a bond of sorts, with Varys providing him with information and advice. He tells Tyrion he has heard that Cersei was responsible for trying to have him killed during the Battle of Blackwater Bay, but is keen to stress they are only whispers. While they are discussing this Varys begins to open a large crate and tells Tyrion of how he became a eunuch.

Varys informs him a sorcerer was responsible for his castration as he needed his genitals for a spell. He then threw him out onto the street to die but Varys says he was determined to live so one day he could have his revenge. He finishes opening the crate as he says this to reveal the elderly sorcerer gagged inside. He tells Tyrion to bide his time, he will get his revenge.

Varys also make use of Ros, a prostitute, to spy on Littlefinger (Lord Petyr Baelish), who tells Varys how his rival is obsessed with Sansa Stark and may be making plans to help her escape. Ros's actions are later discovered by Petyr and he gives her to Joffrey to kill. Throughout the series Varys and Littlefinger are seen consistently verbally sparring as they attempt to outdo each other.

Varys tells Tyrion that his father knows who Shae really is and that he must persuade her to leave. However he is later ordered by Cersei to take part in the trial when Tyrion is accused of murdering Joffrey. Varys is called as a witness for Cersei instead of vouching for Tyrion. His features throughout suggest he doesn't want to be testifying against his trusted friend.

Varys assists Jamie in helping Tyrion escape his death sentence and waits for him by a ship. Finally Tyrion arrives and Varys assumes the escapee has done something, as he hurries him into a crate on board. These suspicions are confirmed when he hears the Kings Landing bells ring out, signifying Tywin Lannister's death, and he makes the decision to also climb aboard the ship.

Petyr Baelish (Littlefinger)

He may seem like a minor character initially; even inconsequential. But the audience will slowly learn that it is Littlefinger who has started the game of thrones and is intent on winning.

The brothel owner and expert manipulator initially acts as an ally to Ned Stark, who believes Littlefinger is still in love with Catelyn. He keeps providing Ned with information and when Robert dies, suggests that they keep Joffrey on the throne while they rule the realm. Ned dismisses this as treachery and asks Petyr to get the City Watch on his side. However,

Littlefinger turns on Ned and has the City Watch arrest him, which ultimately ends in Ned's execution.

Tyrion attempts to find out who from Littlefinger, Varys and the Grand Maester Pycelle is acting as a spy for Cersei. He promises each of them great rewards if they assist him with the plans. For Littlefinger he is told that he'll be made Lord of Harrenhaal and Riverlands. He does this telling each of the three men different marriage plans for the Queen's daughter Mrycella. When Cersei confronts Tyrion about Mrycella being betrothed to a young boy in House Martell, Pycelle reveals himself to be the spy. Littlefinger is furious about the deception but Tyrion placates him by offering him the chance to act as a representative and meet Catelyn to offer an exchange.

At the time Catelyn is at Renly's camp trying to urge him to support Robb. He reaches the camp and meets Catelyn, offering her the safe return of Sansa and Arya if she releases Jamie. While there he also makes an unsuccessful pass at her.

Petyr then turns to Renly and offers to help him win the throne, but Renly dies before a decision can be reached. He then negotiates an alliance between the wealthy Tyrells and Lannister's, which helps them to win the Battle of Blackwater against Stannis. When Petyr discovers that Sansa is to be married into the Tyrell family, he immediately informs Tywin and Cersei, who have her married to Tyrion. For all his work he is finally mad Lord of Harrenhaal.

Littlefinger begins to take a liking to Sansa, commenting to her how much she reminds him of her mother and that he wants to help her escape. The manipulative games he thrives on then unfolds. He proposes a marriage to the widow Lysa Arryn of the Vale and has plans to bring Sansa with him as he knows she will be a far more politically powerful partner. Varys's spy, Ros, discovers this and informs him. To stop Littlefingers plans to move up the ladder Varys then manages to convince Lady Olenna Tyrell that a marriage between her grandson, Ser Loras and Sansa would be a good thing.

Cersei asks Littlefinger to find out information on the Tyrells and he sends one of his male prostitutes to seduce the homosexual Loras. Loras tells the prostitute of the upcoming marriage plans and who relays this to Baelish. Littlefinger then asks Sansa if she will join him on the ship and when she refuses realizes Varys's work. Petyr tells the Lannister's of the plans and in response, they arrange for Sansa to marry Tyrion, to keep her and her close to them. Littlefinger also realizes it was Ros who betrayed him and so gives her to Joffrey who tortures and then kills her.

After Joffrey is killed, Petyr has Sansa whisked away on a boat to the Vale, where he intends to marry Catelyn's sister, Lysa Arryn. He confesses to Sansa that he and his accomplice, Lady Olenna Tyrell had Joffrey killed as he could not be trusted. At the Vale, the audience finds out that it was also Petyr who convinced Lysa to poison her husband and then tell Catelyn that it was the Lannister's who killed Jon, ultimately creating a situation for the civil war. With Sansa pretending to be his niece he then weds Lady Lysa.

Lady Arryn's child, Robin, ruins Sansa's building of Winterfell that she makes in the snow and upset, she slaps him. Littlefinger calms her before she demands to know more about why he had Joffrey killed. Littlefinger tells her he did so because of his love for her mother, before telling her she is more beautiful than Catelyn ever was. He leans in and kisses her, something Lady Arryn witnesses. An enraged Lysa tries to throw Sansa out of the moon door before being stopped by Baelish. He tells her that he's always loved one woman, her sister and then pushes Lysa to her death.

Littlefinger is then questioned by the Lords of the Vale about Lysa's death which says was suicide, something they don't believe because of her love for her son. Littlefinger is visibly concerned when Sansa enters to give her testimony, however, she backs up his story and confirms she jumped to her death and the Lords are convinced. Later, he asks Sansa why she supported him, to which she replies that if he is killed then she would have no idea what the Lords will then want from her, however, she knows what he wants. He then see's her later with, darker hair wearing a low-cut dress and the pair share a smile.

Sandor Clegane

Sandor Clegane, also known as the Hound, is a member of the Kingsguard and a private bodyguard of Joffrey Baratheon. He is also the younger brother of The Mountain, Gregor Clegane.

Even though he is initially portrayed as a brute, the audience is soon shown that the Hound is a more complex character than initially perceived as he has moments of compassion. Due to an incident in his childhood that left his face badly burnt he has a deep fear of fire, which comes into play during the Battle of Blackwater.

When Joffrey is enjoying showing Sansa her fathers head and has struck for implying Robb may win the war Sandor notices that she is thinking about pushing Joffrey to his death. However, he saves her, and Joffrey's, life when he steps in to offer her a handkerchief for her bloodied lip. He saves Sansa again during the riots when a group of men hold her attack her with the intention of raping and killing her.

When Wildfire is used in the battle, a terrified Sandor abandons the fight and leaves King's Landing. He tries to convince Sansa to come with him as he will guarantee her safety, but she refuses, wrongly believing that Stannis is set to win the battle. Sandor then leaves.

He is then captured by the Brotherhood Without Banners, who also have Arya Stark with him, and he is given a trial by combat in order to answer for his crime in killing Arya's friend. His opponent uses magic to light his sword on fire but a fearful Sandor manages to overcome this. He wins the battle and leaves, also taking Arya as a hostage.

He plans to enlist with Robb Stark in exchange for his sister. When they reach the Twin, where Robb is present, he realizes that the Frey's are massacring the Starks and escapes with Arya. He then decides to try and ransom Arya off to Lady Lysa and makes his way towards the Vale.

When Arya is treating a bite wound he suffers during a fight he tells her what happened to his face. He says as a child he was playing with a toy left by his older brother, Gregor, without his permission. When Gregor returned, without warning he stuck his face into the fire and only stops when servants pulled him off. The Hound says the worst thing about it is that it was his brother that did it and how his father protected Gregor by covering it up.

Sandor and Arya reach Lady Arryn only to be told she is dead. The reaction of the pair is priceless as The Hound looks bewildered and Arya bursts out laughing at continuation of the bad luck. During there time together the pair have formed an uneasy alliance with many of their scenes providing some both drama and some very funny moments.

After failing again to ransom Arya to her family, the pair come across Brienne of Tarth and her squire, Podrick. A fight ensues between Brienne and The

Hound over who should be the guardian for Arya, with Brienne already looking for her sister Sansa and Sandor unwilling to give up his payday. Brienne wins the fight, hitting him rock and knocking him down a small cliff. Arya finds him badly wounded and he begs her to kill him, even taunting her. Arya refuses to though and simply takes his coins and walks away leaving the fate of The Hound unknown.

Margaery Tyrell

Beautiful, cunning, ambitious and compassionate, Margeary Tyrell possesses all the attributes required in becoming a successful queen.

Margeary is initially married to Renly Baratheon, but the marriage does not last long as Renly is killed soon after. She persuades her brother; Ser Loras that they should leave before Stannis arrives to take over Renly's troops. She is then betrothed to Joffrey Baratheon after the Tyrells help the Lannister's win the Battle of Blackwater.

Her relationship with Cersei contains friction, as Cersei finds her as a competitor instead of a daughter-in-law, especially due to the fact that Margaery has the support of the common folk, something the Lannister's lack. She also develops a friendship with Sansa, while increasing her influence over Joffrey as well. The control she seems to have over Joffrey is of particular concern to Cersei.

Margaery comments to Cersei that they will be sisters with the upcoming marriages of Tyrion and Sansa's, and Cersei and Ser Loras. Cersei is unimpressed, reminding her of the story of "Rains of Castamere" and the complete destruction of House Reyne after they crossed the Lannister's. An obvious warning to Margaery and the Tyrells that they can expect the same if they conspires against her family.

She finally weds Joffrey, only for him to die after being poisoned during the Royal Wedding. Margaery then starts to seduce Tommen before Cersei can poison him against her.

Bronn

Bronn is a dangerous and skilled fighter, and makes use of his abilities by working as a sellsword for Tyrion Lannister.

When Tyrion is given a trial by combat at the Vale in order to prove his innocence in attempting to kill Bran he nominates Bronn as his champion. He defeats the champion nominated by Lady Lysa and following his release, Tyrion keeps Bronn with him to be his personal bodyguard.

It is Bronn, who finds Tyrion a prostitute named Shae in King's Landing, with whom Tyrion eventually falls in love. He is later made the commander of the City Watch by Tyrion, who himself becomes acting Hand of the King.

During the Battle of Blackwater, Bronn shoots a flaming arrow into the ship containing Wildfire, with the resulting explosion destroying much of Stannis's fleet. He also saves Sandor Clegane's life by when the latter freezes at the sight of fire. After the battle Bronn receives a knighthood as a result of his exploits but is removed as commander of the City Watch when

Tywin takes the role of Hand of the King back from Tyrion.

After Jamie Lannister loses his hand, Tyrion has Bronn practice sparring with Jamie in private so that Jamie can learn to fight with his left hand. Initially, Bronn easily bests him at first using underhanded attacks, but the Jamie noticeably improves over time. After one training session he beseeches Jamie to visit his brother who is being held, suspected of killing Joffrey.

Cersei bribes Bronn with an offer marriage into a wealthy and important family if he refuses to fight for Tyrion against Gregor Clegane in his trial by combat. Bronn goes to see Tyrion and tells him this as well as doubting his chances if he were to fight the Mountain. He admits that one mistake against the giant would mean death and when he weighs it versus the marriage opportunity; he claims it isn't worth the risk. Tyrion is sad to hear this but says he understands. The pair says farewell and Tyrion remarks it is looking like he will have to kill Gregor himself, noting it would make a great song. Bronn departs by saying he hopes he hears it one day.

Shae

Shae is a prostitute, with whom Tyrion falls in love and the two start a relationship.

She is introduced to Tyrion by Bronn, and the two eventually fall in love. However, problems start to emerge when Tywin discovers that Tyrion has a prostitute and forbids him to take Shae to the court. Tyrion still manages to smuggle her in, with only Varys being able to find out. She is then promoted to the position of Sansa's handmaiden, so that no one will be aware of the relationship between her and Tyrion.

Even though the two keep meeting secretly, friction develops when Tyrion is married to Sansa, with Shae refusing to sleep with Tyrion after he weds Sansa. Varys offer hers a new life across the Narrow Sea and gives her diamonds as a parting gift, but she refuses to leave unless Tyrion requests her to.

Tyrion then starts to refuse her advances as he is now married and the two argue after her latest attempt to seduce him fails. The words exchanged are overheard by a spy acting for Cersei and they go to tell her about Shae immediately. Cersei spots Shae and points her out to Tywin during the wedding breakfast for Joffrey and Margaery and he tells her he wants to see Shae before the wedding. Tyrion then tells Shae to leave the kingdom as she is in great danger and has Bronn send her on a ship, and she runs away in tears. When he asks Bronn whether Shae boarded the ship, Bronn assures him that she did. He then asks Bronn if he saw the ship sail away to which Bronn reassures him that no one was watching him escort her to the ship.

Shae appears as the final witness in Tyrion's trial and has clearly been prepared by Cersei or her subordinates. She claims that he kidnapped her and forced her to become his whore, while she also says that she witnessed Tyrion and Sansa planning Joffrey's death. A devastated Tyrion begs her to stop, but after having his heart broken is unable to stop himself launching a vicious verbal attack on everyone in attendance before demanding a trial by combat.

After Tyrion escapes his jail he goes to kill his father before boarding his getaway ship. He is stunned to see Shae lying in Tywins bed and strangles her. He apologizes to her corpse and continues looking for his father.

Brienne of Tarth

An exceptionally skilled fighter, Brienne of Tarth's bravery is only surpassed by her unwavering loyalty.

She defeats Ser Loras Tyrell at a tournament hosted by Renly Baratheon, after which is admitted as a member of his Kingsguard. She is with Renly and Catelyn when the Shadow swoops in and kills Renly. She then runs away with Catelyn and takes an oath of fealty towards Catelyn. When Catelyn releases Jamie, she instructs Brienne to make sure Jamie does not slip away.

As Jamie and Brienne travel, Jamie continually taunts her in the hope of engaging him in a fight thereby giving him an opportunity to escape. She refuses to take the bait though and impresses Jamie withy her sword skills when dealing with three Stark soldiers who recognize the Kingslayer.

Jamie finally manages to engage Brienne in battle, but loses. As soon as the battle ends, they are taken by a man named Locke from House Bolton. Jamie tries to warn Brienne that the men are going to rape her and if she wants to live to not put up a fight. She simply states that she will fight even it means she is killed. Back at the camp, Locke and his men are indeed about to rape Brienne, however, Jamie intervenes, making up fables to convince the men that they can earn a huge fortune in exchange for Brienne, though his continued efforts at bartering with Locke lose Jamie his right-hand. While both are held captive they become closer, with Jamie even confiding in Brienne why he had to kill the Mad King.

When Roose Bolton arrives and releases Jamie, Roose decides to keep Brienne for abetting treason. Jamie then returns to rescue Brienne, only to find out she has been thrown in a pit to fight a bear. Jamie jumps in the pit and rescues Brienne from the bear.

At King's Landing, Jamie is reminded by Brienne of his promise to Catelyn to return her daughters safely. After Sansa escapes, Jamie sends Brienne to ensure that she remains safe in order to honor his promise to Catelyn. He gives her his sword, which she names "Oathkeeper" and they share a touching goodbye.

Accompanying her as her squire on the quest is Podrick, former assistant to Tyrion Lannister and his savior during the Battle of Blackwater Bay. However, he does not have much experience outside of pouring drinks and proves to be an inconvenience for Brienne.

After deciding to visit the Vale they come across Arya Stark and The Hound. Podrick recognizes The Hound and Brienne tells Arya she will take her to safety though the young Stark girl does not believe her and a fierce battle ensues between Brienne and The Hound. Brienne wins after knocking him down a small cliff but returns to find that Arya has gone.

Gendry

Gendry is one of the many bastards of Robert Baratheon but is initially unaware of this fact.

He decides to join the Night's Watch after realizing he is out of work. However, midway in the travel, the group he is travelling with is accosted by gold cloaks, from King's Landing, who are looking for Gendry, on Joffrey's orders that any bastard of Robert is to be killed. He is captured along with Arya, whom he met on his travels, and they are kept as prisoners. Ser Gregor Clegane's troops are torturing and executing everyone, one-by-one in the hope of finding more information on bastards of Robert, however this is stopped by the arrival of Tywin Lannister who feels they are more valuable kept alive. Eventually, he manages to escape with Arya.

Gendry decides to stay with the Brotherhood Without Banners, who took both him and Arya in with them after their escape from King's Landing. Arya is dismayed by this decision, but before anything else can happen, Melisandre appears and buys off Gendry from the Brotherhood. She then seduces him, only to leech his body to complete a ritual.

Melisandre plans to sacrifice Gendry to her God, but before she is able to carry out her plans, Ser Davos releases Gendry.

Theon Greyjoy

Cocky, arrogant and brash, Theon Greyjoy may have been raised in Winterfell, but his mannerisms always betrayed the truth that he was an Ironborn. Theon Greyjoy grew up at Winterfell after his father led a failed invasion, though was permitted to remain as the Lord of the Iron Islands if Theon became a Ward to the Stark's.

After Ned leaves for King's Landing, Theon advises Robb on how to run Winterfell. When he saves Bran from wildlings, he is scolded by Robb on risking the life of Bran, which Theon does not take well.

When Robb decides to go to war after Ned is killed, Theon supports this and asks Robb if he will let him go to his father and seek the support of the Ironborn. Robb agrees, and Theon leaves for his home, where he receives a cold reception. He tries to seduce a stranger who offers him a ride to the castle, though is less than impressed when it turns out that it is his sister, Yara. His father, Balon Greyjoy is dismissive of his son and rejects Robb's proposal of an alliance.

Theon betrays Robb and attempts to seek the approval of his father, who wants to sack Winterfell while it is poorly defended. Theon disobeys his father and takes over Winterfell. When Bran and Rickon abandon Winterfell, Theon burns two peasant boys and passes them off as Bran and Rickon, threatening to destroy anyone else who challenges him.

His sister Yara arrives at Winterfell and tells Theon to abandon the place as everyone in the North wants to kill him for what he supposedly did to Bran and

Rickon. Theon refuses to leave and prepares to fight Ramsay Bolton's forces, which had been sent by Robb Stark to regain Winterfell. Theon is betrayed by his own men, who allow Ramsay to enter, only to be flayed alive by Ramsay's men.

Ramsay then imprisons Theon and subjects him to cruel torture, which includes prying off his fingernails and driving a nail through his foot. He also ends up cutting of Theon's penis and sends it to his sister. The torture and the humiliation completely break Theon, who now refers to himself as Reek and is shown to be completely subservient to Ramsay Bolton.

Ramsey sends Theon's penis to his father with a letter demanding that they remove all of their forces from the north; otherwise they should expect more of Theon's body parts. Balon Greyjoy says Theon has been a fool for not following his orders and as he can no longer heir means nothing to him. Yara is more concerned though and against her fathers wishes sets sail to rescue Theon.

Yara and her group of Iron born troops manage to secretly breach the castle where Theon is being held. They find him being held in a kennel and Reek is steadfast in his refusal to come with her and abandon his master. Ramsey and guards soon arrive and unable to convince her brother that he is Theon, not Reek is forced to leave and escape. Ramsey gives Reek a bath to reward him for his loyalty.

Ramsey tells Reek that he needs him to be someone who he's not, Theon, in order to help him retake Moat Cailan which the Greyjoy's are holding. Reek enters Moat Cailan to deliver the message and sees the troops are struggling and rife with disease and corpses. He tells the commander that he is Theon Greyjoy and he has been kept a prisoner at House Bolton. He tells them to surrender peacefully and they will be allowed to go home safely. The commander rejects the offer and insults him for being weak and not a true Ironborn. Reek is unnerved by this attack and is on the verge of breaking down before one of the commander's men puts an axe in his superiors head. And tells Reek they accept the terms. Ramsey and his men promptly massacre and flay them all anyway.

Oberyn Martell

Prince Oberyn Martell of House Martell quickly became a firm favorite with viewers. With his impressive fighting skills, his insatiable appetite for sex and his verbal duels with the Lannister's, Oberyn made quite the impact.

Also known as The Red Viper, he arrives at Kings Landing in place of his reigning older brother, Prince Doran, representing of House Martell for the wedding of Joffrey and Margaery. Tyrion is awaiting the arrival of the Martells in order to welcome them but is told Oberyn arrived in the city before dawn. Tyrion quickly realizes he will be already enjoying the local brothels.

Oberyn and his wife are taking there pick for male and female company when he hears two Lannister guards sing their House song. He becomes enraged and gets into a fight with them, stabbing one through the wrist before Tyrion arrives to disrupt the fight to talk to the Red Viper.   They leave the brothel and Tyrion asks why he has come to Kings Landing. Oberyn then tells him how Ser Gregor Clegane was responsible for raping his sister before murdering her and her children. He says that the Lannister's are not the only ones who always repay debts.

Oberyn and his wife partake in an orgy and one of the brothels before being interrupted by another Lannister, this time Tywin. The two of them talk about Oberyn's love of poisons then Tywin asks him to be a judge for Tyrion's trial. Oberyn initially refuses saying he holds Tywin responsible for what happened with his sister, though changes his mind when he is offered a seat on the small council and that Tywin will arrange it so he can Gregor Clegane. The Hand of the King also makes it clear he wishes to reunite the Houses for if or when Daenerys invades with her dragons.

During Tyrion's trial Oberyn questions sporadically witnesses, including Shae, though he does this mainly to amuse himself. When the trial ends dramatically with Tyrion demanding a trial by combat Oberyn seems intrigued. After Jamie and Bronn refuse to fight for Tyrion, Oberyn visits him. He recounts a tale of when he first met him when Tyrion had just been born. He states that Cersei had made a grand show of the monster he was about to see but all he saw was a baby.

Oberyn states again that he wants justice for his sister but Tyrion tells him he will not find any in Kings Landing. He disagrees and says it is the perfect place to for him to get justice for his sister and offers to fight as Tyrion's champion opposite The Mountain, Ser Gregor Clegane.

Before the battle Tyrion is worried by Oberyn's lack of armor as well as the fact he's drinking. He dismisses this by saying it's what he always does and heavy armor will hamper his fighting abilities.

The fight begins and Oberyn's quick and agile movement causes problems for The Mountain. Well dodging attacks and landing minor wounds Oberyn screams for his opponent to admit that he raped and murdered his sister. Clegane begins to tire chasing his adversary and Oberyn stabs him in the stomach before slicing at his hamstring. Clegane falls to his knees in pain as he is easily outmaneuvered by the skillful Red Viper.

Oberyn thrusts his spear through Clegane's breastplate and the giant falls to his back coughing up blood. Oberyn yells again for him to admit he committed the heinous acts against his sister and reveal who was behind it, as he points his spear at Tywin. However, as he moves to deliver the final blow, Clegane surprisingly trips him and smashes him in the face with his huge fist, knocking out several teeth. Clegane gouges Oberyn's eyes out with his thumbs and as Oberyn is screaming in agony, roars that he raped her, killed the children and then killed her by smashing her head into the floor. Clegane then does the same to Oberyn killing him instantly in perhaps the most violent death in Game of Thrones so far. Tywin then sentences Tyrion to death.

White Walkers

Perhaps the most mysterious, and dangerous characters in Game of Thrones are the White Walkers.

During a bitterly cold winter that lasted many years the White Walkers headed south and destroyed everything in their path. The whole of Westeros united to drive the White Walkers back to the farthest part of the north and the Wall was erected to make sure they were kept out.

We see them in the opening scenes of the first episode as they massacre some Wildlings, leaving the bodies as a warning. They can also reanimate corpses, called Wight's, in order to serve them.

The Nights Watch are informed that the Wildlings past the Wall are claiming the White Walkers have returned. When Tyrion visits and talks to Commander Jeor Mormont he notes that there is something ominously growing beyond the Wall and they desperately need supplies with the harsh winter coming and the prospect this threat makes a move. After Jon saves Jeor from a Wight he decides that the Nights Watch is going beyond the Wall to investigate and tells Jon that the war for the throne in the south pales in comparison to the White Walkers return.

Jon see's Craster leaving a baby boy down in the woods near to his Keep, and a large figure with bright blue eyes arrives and picks the baby up before leaving. Later in the series we see the same thing happen when Night's Watch mutineer Rast leaves a baby and the White Walker carries him back to a frozen and mysterious place. He places the baby on an altar and another, approaches touching the baby on the face. The baby immediately turns into a White Walker.

Conclusion

Now that you have completed this character description guide, I hope that you have a good understanding of the Game of Thrones, and now you can be the expert and understand the TV series. I hope that this guide served to show the variety and complexity of the various characters that combine together to create a compelling storyline.

The Game of Thrones universe is full of morally ambiguous people who will do anything to increase or sustain their wealth and power. Although few and far between, there are some good characters who attempt to look towards the greater good instead of their own personal gain.